Phonics Fun
ACTIVITY BOOK

Reading and Writing Activities for Kids

Brian P. Cleary

LernerClassroom ◆ Minneapolis

LernerClassroom
An imprint of Lerner Publishing Group, Inc.
241 First Avenue North
Minneapolis, MN 55401 USA

For reading levels and more information, look up this title at www.lernerbooks.com.

Main body text set in Mikado a Regular.
Typeface provided by HVD Fonts.

Manufactured in the United States of America
1-51319-50290-3/30/2022

Table of Contents

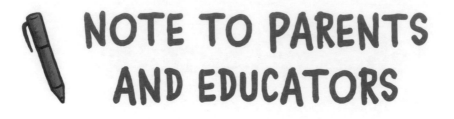

NOTE TO PARENTS AND EDUCATORS

Dear Parents and Educators,

As a former adult literacy coach and the father of three children, I know that learning to read isn't always easy. That's why I developed the *Phonics Fun Activity Book: Reading and Writing Activities for Kids*. The activities in this book employ a combination of devices to help children learn to read. They use rhyme, repetition, illustration, and phonics to introduce young readers to sounds, letter combinations, and word endings that will improve reading knowledge and confidence.

The bridge to literacy is one of the most important we will ever cross. It's my hope that the *Phonics Fun Activity Book* will help new readers to hop, gallop, and skip from one side to the other!

Sincerely,

NOTE TO READERS

Dear Readers,

The activities in this book are all about reading. They explore letters and sounds that will help you read. The activities are also fun! You will laugh and smile as you learn.

Brian P. Cleary

Short Vowel Sounds

Vowels are sounds in words. The letters **a**, **e**, **i**, **o**, and **u** are vowels. You can hear short vowel sounds in words like **fun** and **cat**.

Switch That Sound!

Look at the list of words below. Change each short vowel sound to create new words! For example, you can change **bit** to **bat** by changing the letter **i** to an **a**.

Use these letters to make new words with short vowel sounds: **a**, **e**, **i**, **o**, and **u**.

bit changes to **b__t**

fun changes to **f__n**

cat changes to **c__t**

men changes to **m__n**

fox changes to **f__x**

Write a sentence using some of your new words.

_____

_____

_____

✏ See and Spell

Spell out the objects and animals in the pictures using the list of letters. Use each letter once. The words you spell will all have short vowel sounds!

n b g l p t s a i l u e o n l g

_ _ _

_ _ _

_ _ _

_ _ _

_ _ _ _

 Draw It!

The words **can**, **net**, **kid**, **mom**, and **sun** all have short vowel sounds. Think of a word for an animal that has a short vowel sound. Draw the animal. Next to your picture, write the word. Circle the short vowel sound.

What are your favorite things to eat? Can you think of a food word that has a short vowel sound? Draw it! Then write the word and circle the short vowel sound.

Think about objects you see at home and at school. Can you think of objects that have short vowel sounds? Draw them! Then write the words and circle the short vowel sounds.

Short Vowel Sounds with Consonant Blends

Consonants are letters that are not vowels. A consonant blend is when two consonants are side by side in a word. The word **blend** has the short vowel sound **e**. It also has the consonant blends **bl–** and **–nd**.

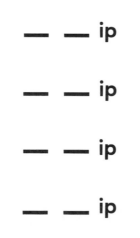 Build a Word!

Look at the list of consonant blends. Add a consonant blend from the list to the short vowel sound **–ip**. Some of the consonant blends will create new words with **–ip**, and others will not. For example, **tr–** added to **–ip** is **trip**.

> **tr sn sw sl gr st fl dr cl sp bl**

— — ip

— — ip

— — ip

— — ip

Super bonus! Can you write one more?

— — ip

 Order, Please!

Read the word below. Then look at the letters in the word. Can you move the letters around to make a new word that has a short vowel sound and a consonant blend? Use all four letters.

$$\boxed{\text{P A N S}}$$

Hint: Some people write each letter on a small square and move the squares to see if they can make a new word.

— — — —

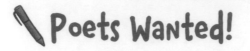 Poets Wanted!

Put on your writer's cap, and finish the rhyming poem. Use some of the words below. All the words have short vowel sounds with consonant blends!

> **swum, drum, flag, brag, brush, crush, dress, press, flop, slop, Fred, sled, grass, glass**

My bedroom had started to stink

from the spilled pizza and drink.

_____

_____

Long Vowel Sounds

A, e, i, o, and **u** are vowels. A long vowel sound is when the vowel sounds like the letter in the alphabet. Many words with a silent **e** at the end have long vowel sounds. For example, the **a** in **bake** is a long vowel sound.

 Rhyme Time!

Look at the list of words below. Each word has a long vowel sound. See if you can write a third word that rhymes for each line. For example, if you have **cake** and **rake**, you can use **t** to make **take**.

Use these letters: t p d b

1. **cake**   2. **rake**   3. — — — —

1. **rose**   2. **hose**   3. — — — —

1. **time**   2. **lime**   3. — — — —

1. **steam**   2. **cream**   3. — — — —

 Poet's Room

Let's make a list of words to use in a fun poem! Read the hints below. Then write what you think the object is. Each word has a long vowel sound.

This is on our face.
It is above our mouth.
We use it to breathe.

1. __ __ __ __

These are on our feet.
Most people have ten.

2. __ __ __ __

We put socks and shoes on these.

3. __ __ __ __

This is where we live.

4. __ __ __ __

It's doing this outside when water falls from the sky.

5. __ __ __ __ __ __ __

This is better than good. It starts with **g**.

6. __ __ __ __ __

This is what people call us. We get it when we are born.

7. __ __ __ __

This is the color of the sky.

8. __ __ __ __

Look at the poem below. Do you see the numbers by the blanks? They are the same numbers from the list you made! Write the word with the same number in the blanks.

I have a soft doggy, and her __ __ , __ __ is Froggy,
7

We got her when she was a puppy.

We also have Kitty, with __ __ , __ __ eyes so pretty,
8

And a lamb and a goat and a guppy.

Froggy nipped at my __ __ , __ __ , my fingers
1

and __ __ , __ __
2

Until Mommy got her some training.

Now she's so sweet, she sits at my __ __ , __ __ ,
3

Sitting close on the porch when it's

__ __ __ __ __ __ __ .
5

When we brought Froggy __ __ , __ __ , she would
4

play, run, and roam,

or chase after a rabbit or mouse.

But now that she's eight, she's turned out so

__ __ __ __ __ .
6

She's my favorite pet in the house.

This poem was written by _____
(your name)

& Brian P. Cleary.

Let's Face It!

Do you see the arrows? They go to three parts of the person's head. Write the parts below. The words for the parts have long vowel sounds!

1. ___ ___ ___ ___

2. ___ ___ ___ ___ ___

3. ___ ___ ___ ___ ___

Long Vowel Sounds with Consonant Blends

An example of a word with a long vowel sound and a consonant blend is **slope**. The long vowel sound **o** sounds like the letter by itself. And **sl–** is a consonant blend.

✏️ Milk Carton Mix-Up!

Look at the word spelled with the milk cartons. Can you think of a new word that has the same letters? Move the letters to find a new word, and write it below. The word will start with a consonant blend and have a long vowel sound.

Hint: The word is what we might have done when we were sad. You'll use one of these consonant blends: **cr, sw, bl**

— — — — —

Pizza Poem!

There are two missing words in the poem below. They start with a consonant blend and have a long vowel sound. They rhyme. Can you help find the missing words?

Hint: The missing words rhyme with **nice**! Use the list of consonant blends below to write new words that rhyme with **nice**. You will use two of these consonant blends:
sl, tr, cl, pr

I love eating pizza,

by the pie or by the __ __ __ __ __ .

And I don't care how much it costs,

'cause I'll pay any __ __ __ __ __ .

✏ See and Spell!

Look at the pictures below. Write the word for the object or animal you see. Each word will have a consonant blend with a long vowel sound.

— — — — —

— — — — —

— — — — —

— — — — —

Super bonus! Look at the words you wrote. Do you see five yellow letters? Write each of the letters in the spaces below to make a new word. The new word has a long vowel sound and a consonant blend. Hint: It's the name of a place where many people speak Spanish.

— — — — —

Short Vowel Sounds with Consonant Digraphs

A consonant digraph is when two consonants make one sound. For example, **ch-** in **chip** is a consonant digraph. The word **chip** also has a short vowel sound.

✏ Winner's Circle!

Look at the pictures below. Write the word for the object next to the picture. Then circle the two words that have a short vowel sound and a consonant digraph. Hint: The short vowel sounds rhyme!

__ __ __ __

__ __ __

__ __ __ __

✏ Let's Act It Out!

Act out the words below. Each word has a short vowel sound with a consonant digraph. You can even ask a friend to act with you!

> **knock**
>
> **sing**
>
> **itch**
>
> **duck**

✏ Rhyme Time!

Read the hints below. Then write a word that goes with the hint. Your words should have short vowel sounds with consonant digraphs.

1. What is another word for bag? The word has four letters. It has a short a sound and ends with a consonant digraph. __ __ __ __

2. What is the opposite of front? The word rhymes with the word from number 1. __ __ __ __

Write a poem with me! Use the words you wrote by the hints to fill in the blanks below.

What insect has eleven teeth,

Is furry and carries a __ __ __ __ ?
₁

Has horns and a tail and some scabs underneath?

I don't know, but there's one on your __ __ __ __ !
₂

Written by Brian P. Cleary &

_____.
(your name)

Long Vowel Sounds with Consonant Digraphs

Shape has a long vowel sound and a consonant digraph. The **a** in **shape** sounds like the letter by itself. The consonants **s** and **h** make one sound, **sh-**.

✎ See and Spell!

Look at the pictures below. Next to each picture, write what you see. Each word you write will have a long vowel sound with a consonant digraph.

Super bonus! Do you see the yellow letters? Write them below. The letters will spell a new word that has a consonant digraph and a long vowel sound.

__ __ __ __

My Teacher, Ms. Olson

Read the hints below. Then write a word that goes with the hint next to each one. Each word will have a consonant digraph and a long vowel sound.

Hint: Each word will end with **-ch**!

1. What does a teacher do? __ __ __ __ __

2. What's the name of the place with water and sand and people? __ __ __ __ __

Use the words to finish the poem below!

Ms. Olson is supersmart,

And she just loves to __ __ __ __ __,
1

But when the summer comes, she likes to

Spend time at the __ __ __ __ __ .
2

Line Dance

Each word from column 1 rhymes with a word from column 2. Draw a line from the word in column 1 to the word it rhymes with in column 2. All the words have long vowel sounds and consonant digraphs.

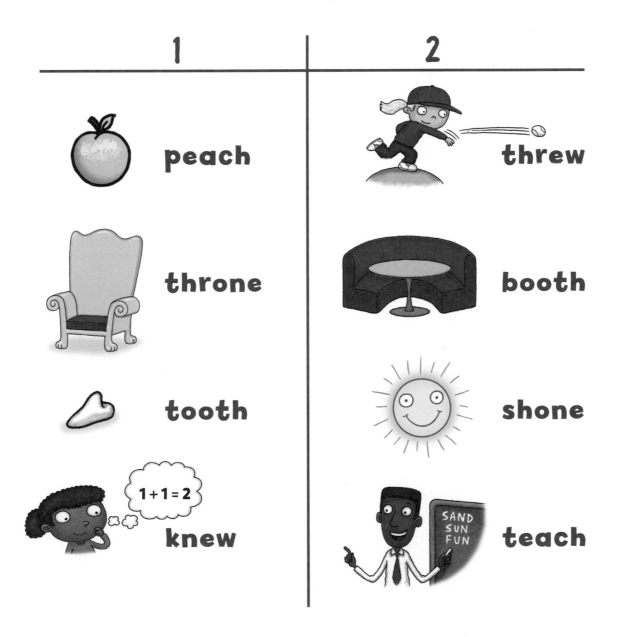

1	2
peach	threw
throne	booth
tooth	shone
knew	teach

Inflectional Endings

An inflectional ending changes what a word means. It can change the time or number of a word. For example, if you add the inflectional ending **–s** to the end of one **cat**, you get many **cats**.

✏ Add an Ending!

Read the words below. Add an inflectional ending to make a new word! Hint: You can add **–s**, **–es**, **–ed**, **–ing**, or **–est**. For example, **run** can change to **running** and **apple** can change to **apples**.

chase   changes to   _____

couch   changes to   _____

draw   changes to   _____

slow   changes to   _____

swim   changes to   _____

Super bonus! Write a sentence using three of the new words you wrote.

_____

_____

_____

Artists Wanted!

Draw the words below. All the words have inflectional endings and short vowel sounds!

witches

clocks

walking

Write a Poem!

Add the inflectional ending **-ing** to the words below:

1. **scoop** changes to __ __ __ __ __ __ __ __

2. **sift** changes to __ __ __ __ __ __ __

Use the words to finish the poem below!

Cleaning the litter box, __ __ __ __ __ __ __ __
                                        ₁

and __ __ __ __ __ __ __,
                    ₂

I gag as I whisper a vow:

I'll never ask my mother or dad

If I can bring home a pet cow!

Diphthongs and R-Controlled Vowels

A diphthong is when two vowels make one sound.
The word **house** has a diphthong.

An r-controlled vowel is when the letter **r** follows a vowel.
The **r** changes how the vowel sounds. The words **car** and
start have r-controlled vowels.

 Changes!

Look at the list of words below. Change the first letter
to make a new word that rhymes. For example, **paw** can
change to **raw.** Each new word will be a diphthong or have
an r-controlled vowel sound.

paw	changes to	__ __ __
tar	changes to	__ __ __
nurse	changes to	__ __ __ __ __
more	changes to	__ __ __ __
joy	changes to	__ __ __

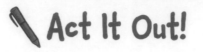

Act It Out!

Read the words below. Each one has a diphthong or an r-controlled vowel sound! Then act out each word. You can even ask a friend to act with you!

shout   **mow**

throw   **cheer**

Super bonus! Write a sentence using some of the words.

_____

_____

_____

✎ Name That Word!

Read the hints below. Then pick the word from the list that goes with each hint. All the words have a diphthong or an r-controlled vowel sound! You will use each word once.

> **mouth   herd   crawl   south   third**

1. When there are a lot of cows in one place, it is called a __ __ __ __ .

2. This comes after second place: __ __ __ __ __ .

3. This is on our face. We use it to talk and sing: __ __ __ __ __ .

4. A baby does this before walking: __ __ __ __ __ .

5. If the word **north** means **up** on a map, then this word means **down**. Hint: It rhymes with the word from number 3: __ __ __ __ __ .

Check out the popular Phonics Fun books!